GARFIELD

F

JIM DAVIS

℞℞
RAVETTE PUBLISHING

First published in 2002 by
Ravette Publishing Limited, Unit 3, Tristar Centre,
Star Road, Partridge Green, West Sussex RH13 8RA

(www.garfield.com)

Printed in Malta by Gutenberg Press

ISBN: 1 84161 145 X

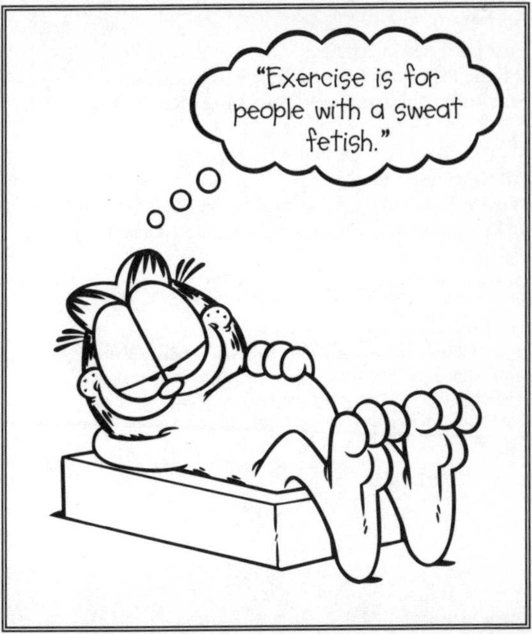
"Exercise is for people with a sweat fetish."

I might as well exercise.
I'm in a bad mood anyway.

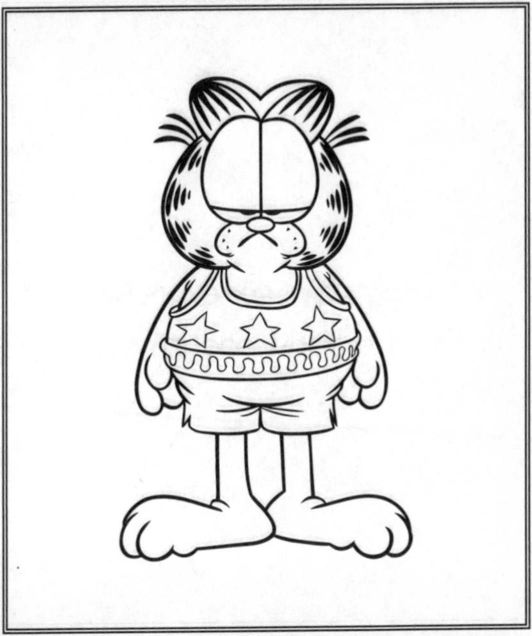

I lose the same pound
every week.

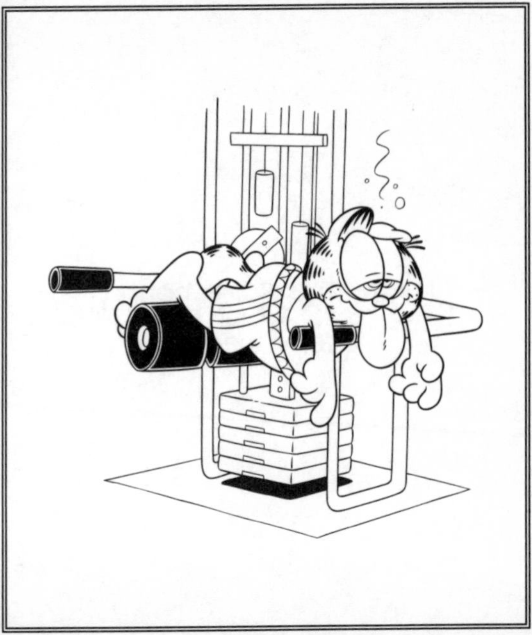

Diet is "Die" with a "T"!

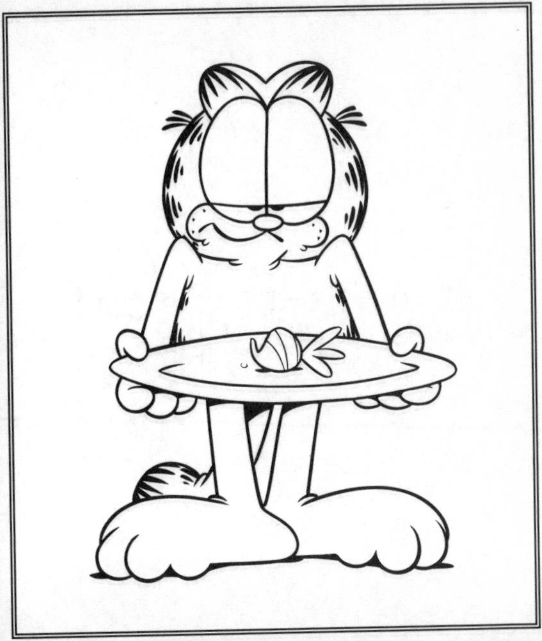

It takes years of neglect
to get a body like this!

One thing about lethargy –
you don't have to work on it!

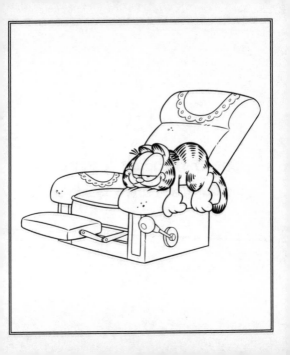

So much for "push".
Tomorrow we work on "up".

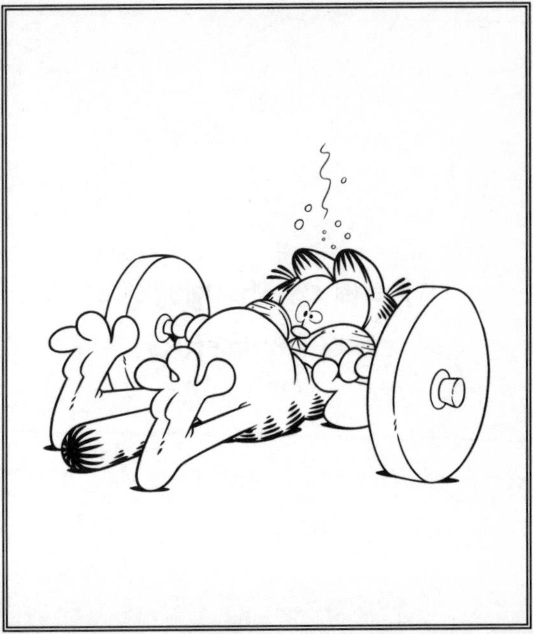

It looks as though I'm on another diet.

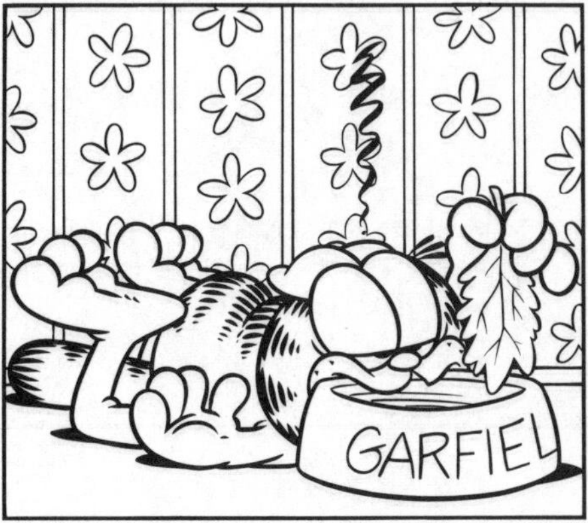
GARFIEL

Stop me before I snack again!

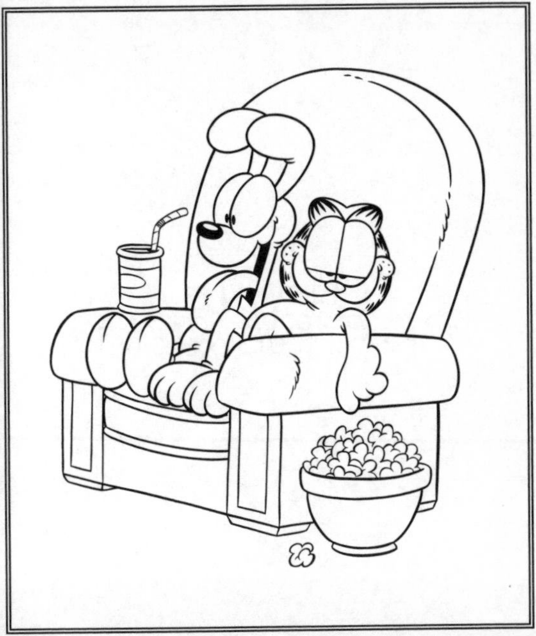

Chewing –
the perfect exercise!

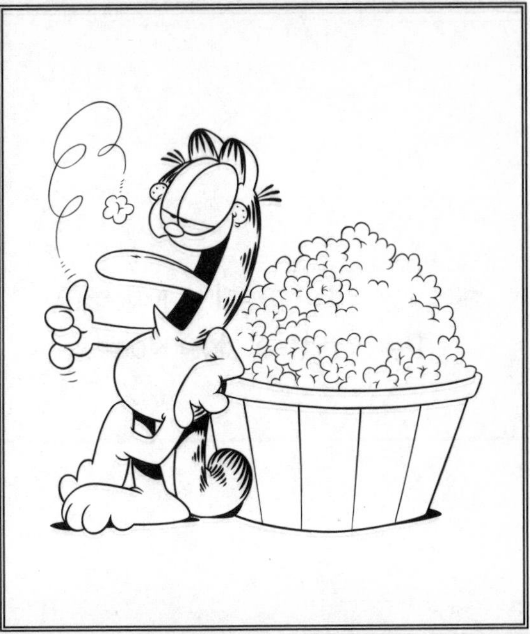

Once my eating gains momentum,
it's hard to slow down.

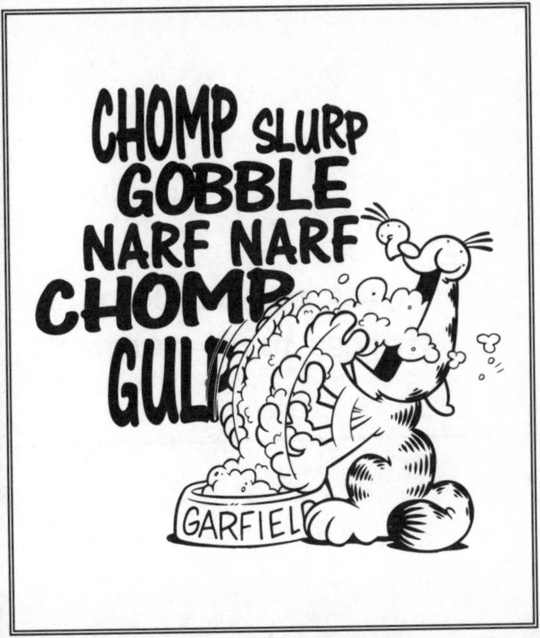
CHOMP SLURP
GOBBLE
NARF NARF
CHOMP
GUL
GARFIEL

Wake me when this
fitness fad is over.

I'm bulking up
for my next diet.

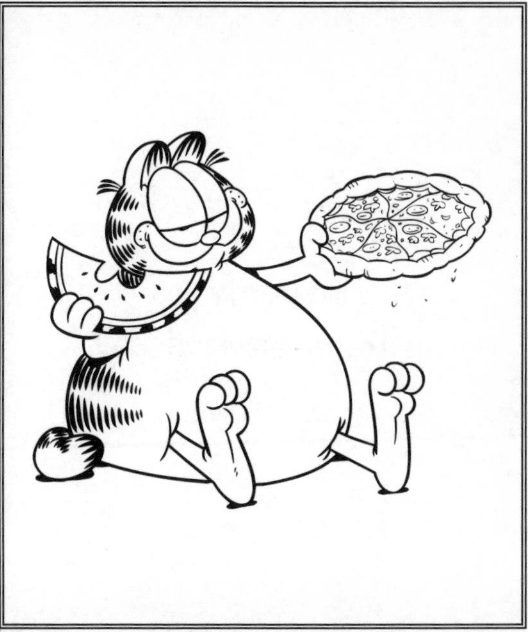

Sweat?
In this classy outfit?!

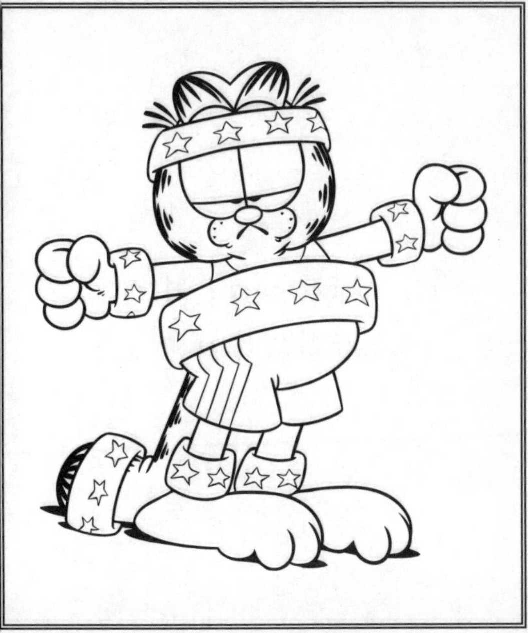

The only thing I stretch
is the truth!

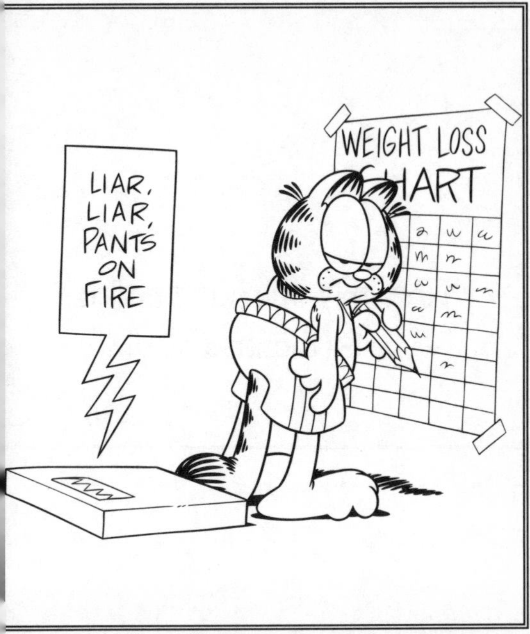
WEIGHT LOSS CHART
LIAR, LIAR, PANTS ON FIRE

Now this is what I call a
well-balanced meal.

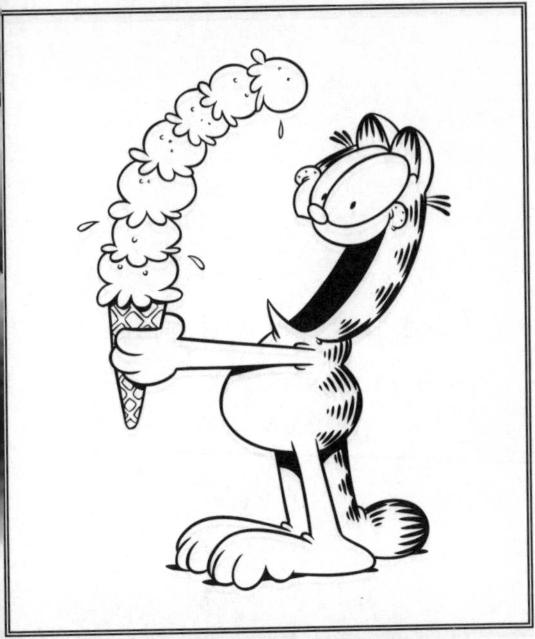

Take this jog and shove it!

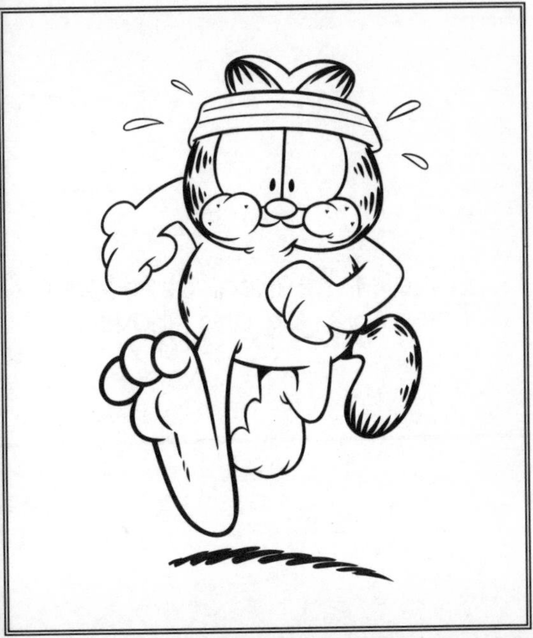

I can't diet for medical reasons –
it makes me hungry!

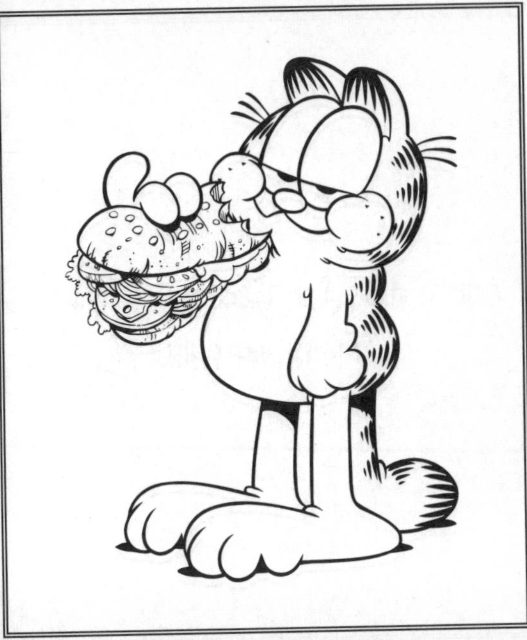

I'm not overweight.
I'm undertall!

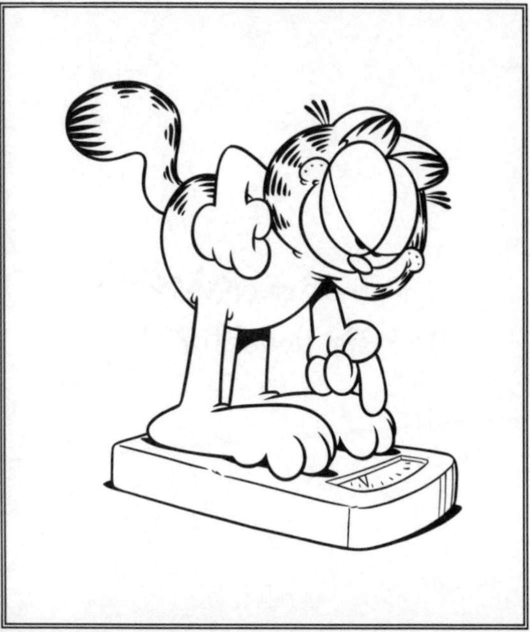

If fitness is so healthy,
why does it hurt so much?

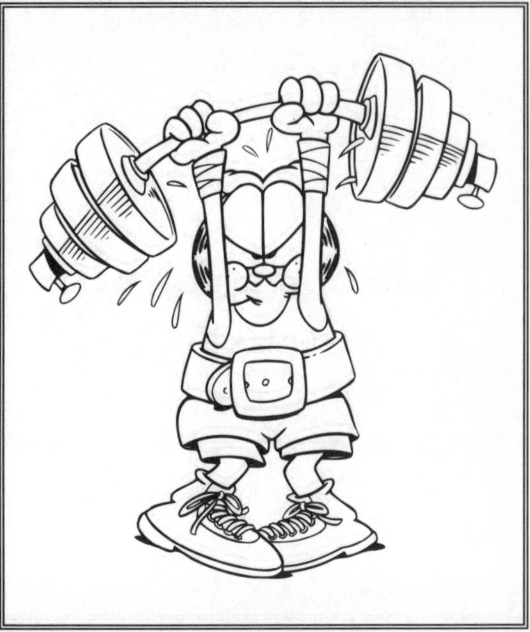

Everything tastes good
on a diet.

I'll procrastinate tomorrow.

Don't ask!!

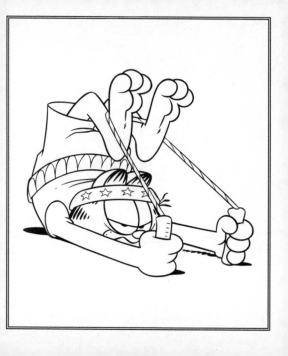

Exercise is for the loafing –
impaired.

I'm not pigging out.
I'm carbo-loading!

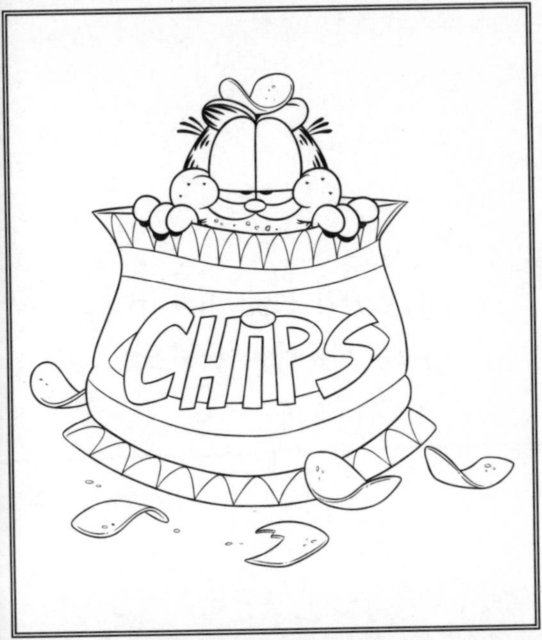
CHIPS

I'll join a gym when they put in a dessert bar.

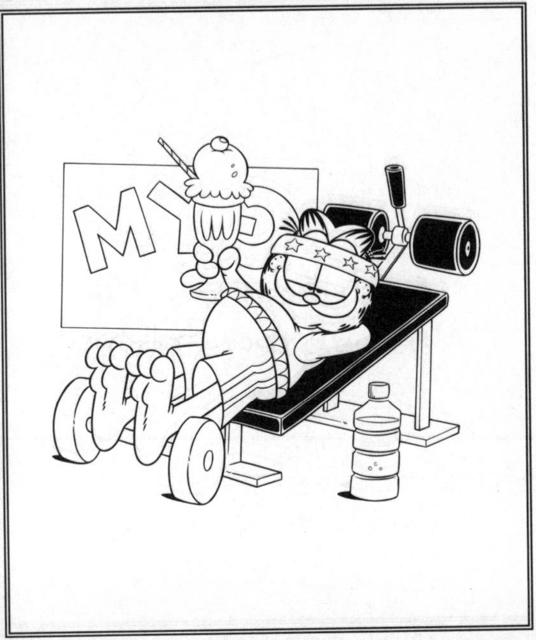

I'm not lazy ...
I'm motivationally challenged!

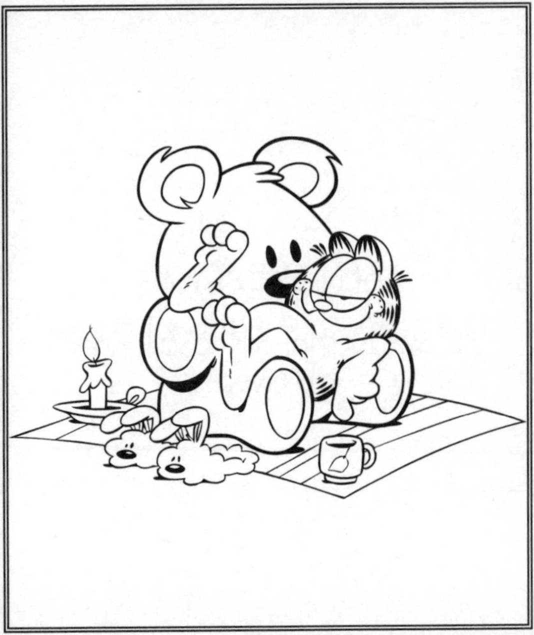

BAN EXERCISE.
Conserve our national supply
of sweat.

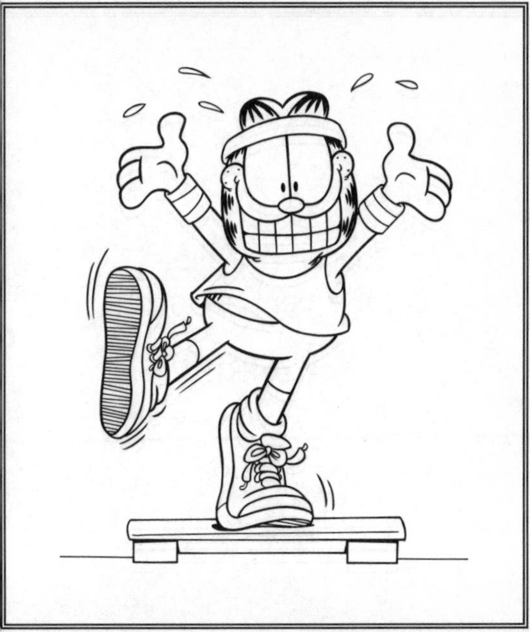

I'm the perfect shape
for my weight.

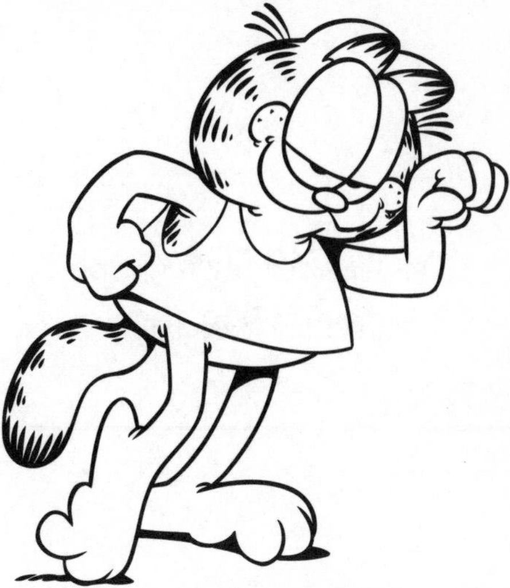

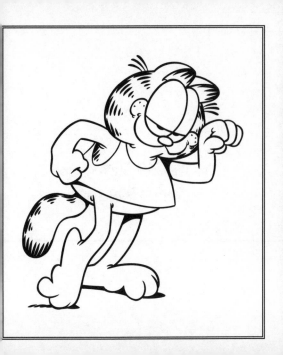

Exercise.
Just skip it.

Most diets
are begun tomorrow.

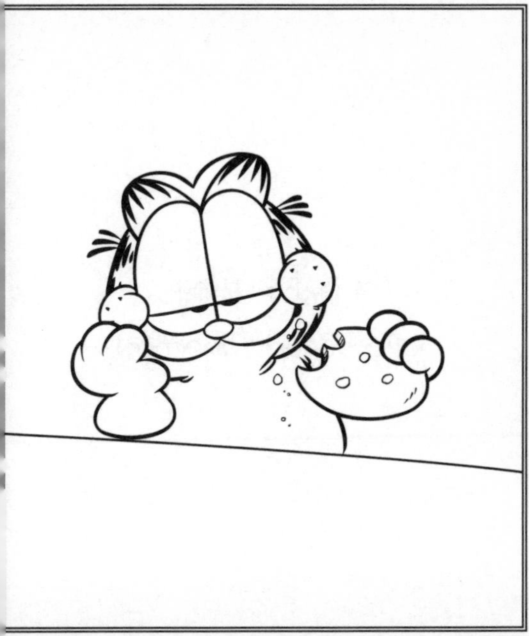

I'm not loafing ...
I'm conserving sweat.

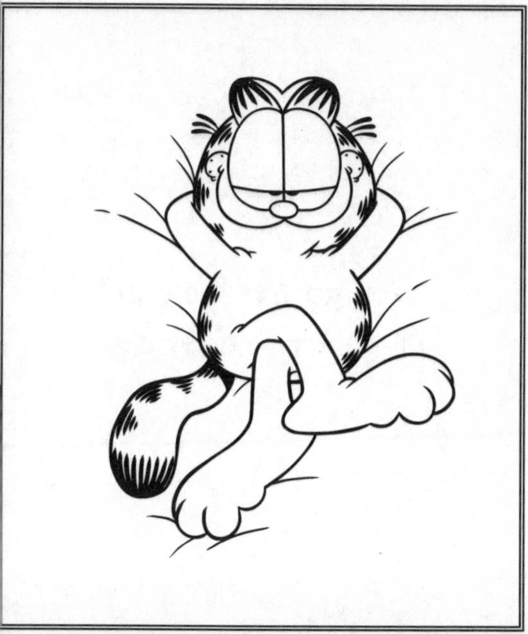

You go for the run.
I'll go for the snacks.

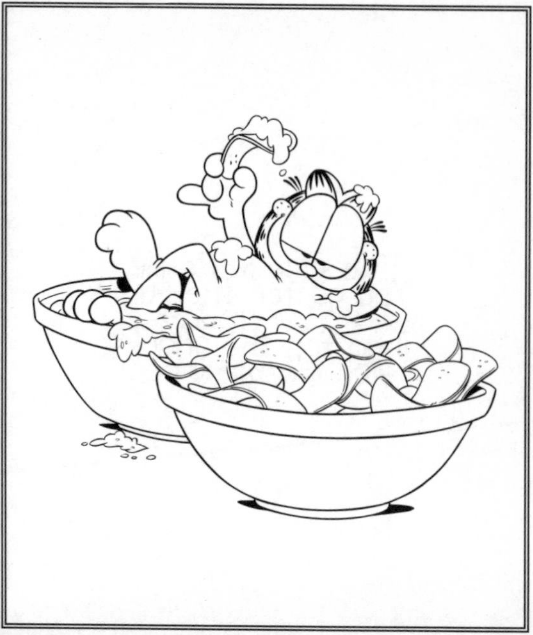

Exercise made me
what I am today ...
sick of exercise!

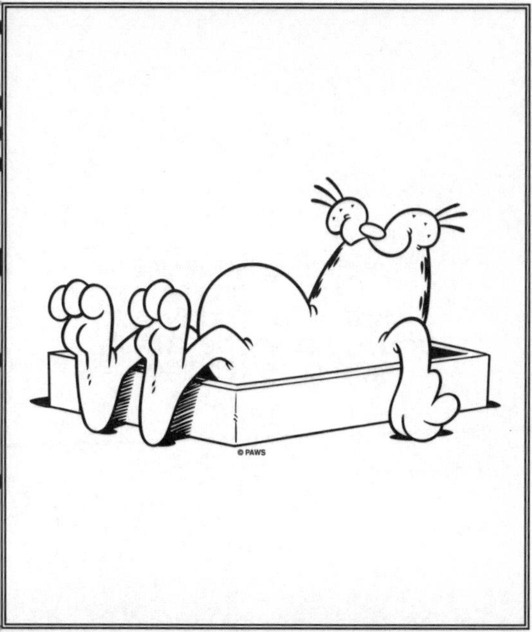
© PAWS

Out of shape
beats no shape at all.

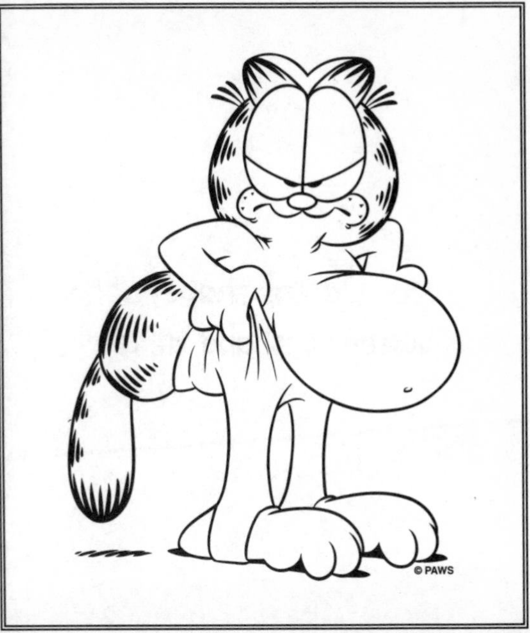
© PAWS

Life is a constant battle
between diet and dessert.

Time for a brisk browse
around the fridge.

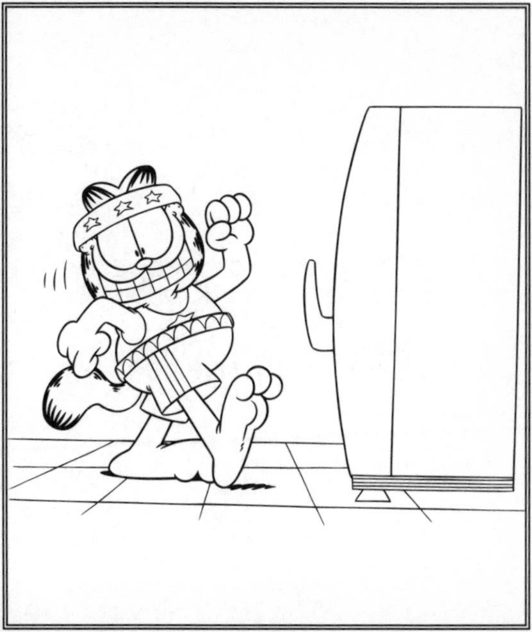

Diets are for people
who want to
belittle themselves.

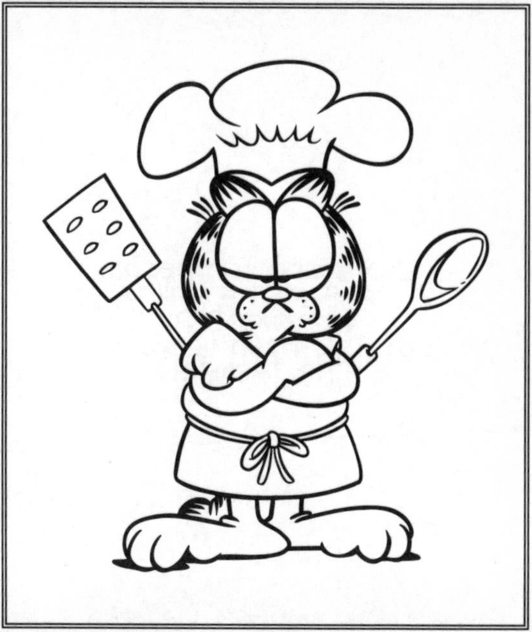

The spirit is willing,
but the flesh is weak.

A diet is too little
of a good thing.

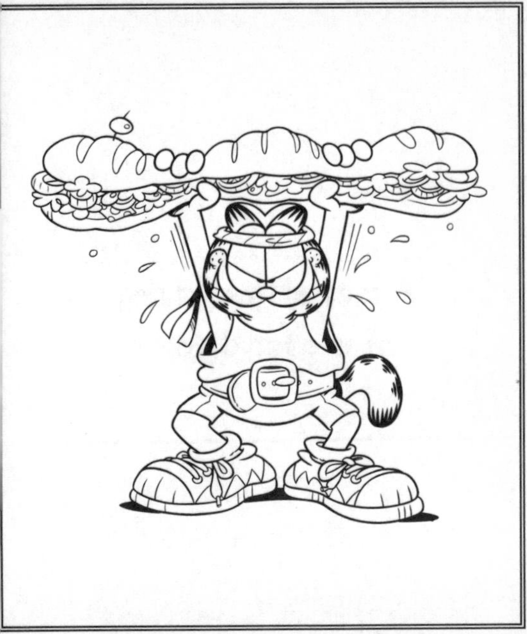

I'm pretty amazing
when I have to be.

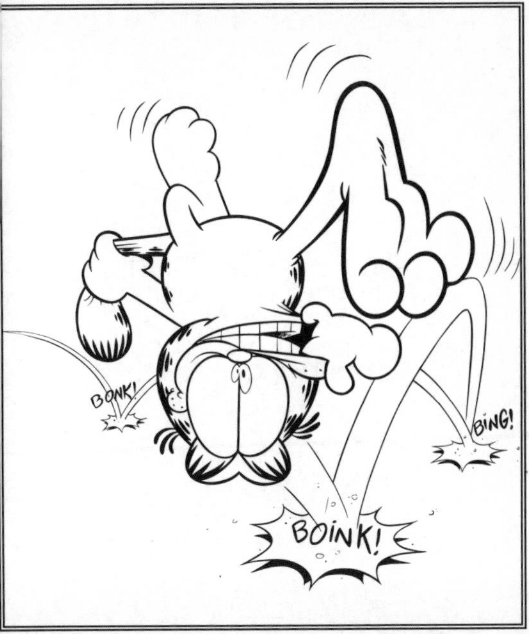
BONK!
BOINK!
BING!

I'm not overweight,
everyone else is
under-nourished.

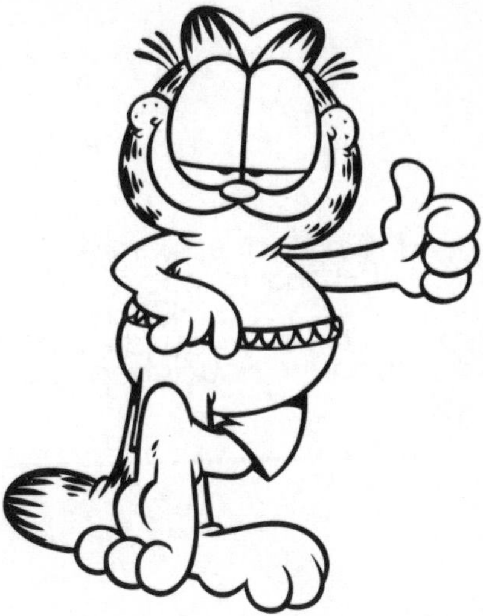

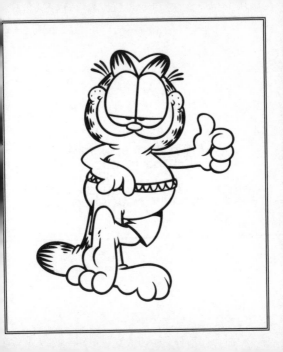

Eating is social.
When you diet, you diet alone.

I don't do sweat.

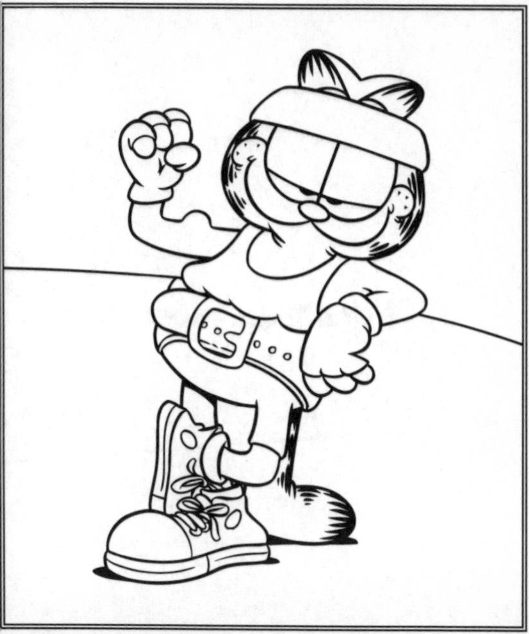

The fridge made me eat it!

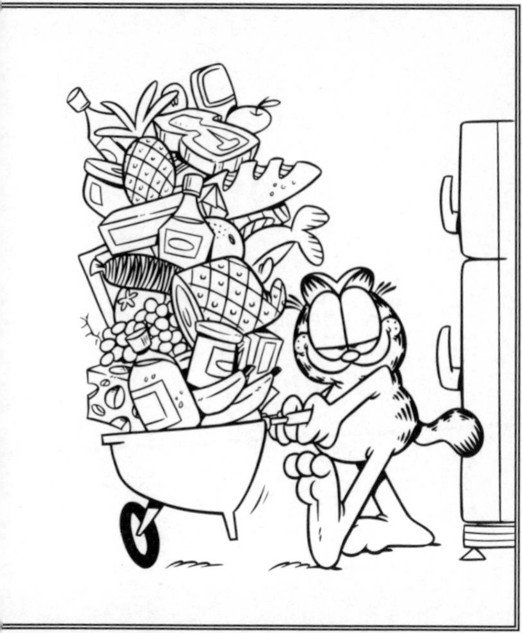

I used to exercise,
but I'm fine now.

I'm not predjudiced.
I hate **all** exercises.

Other books available in this series ...
@ £2.50 each

Garfield's Little Book of Laughs
ISBN: 1 84161 146 8

Garfield's Little Book of Love 'n' Stuff
ISBN: 1 84161 147 2

Garfield's Little Book of Wit 'n' Wisdom
ISBN: 1 84161 148 4

RR

RAVETTE PUBLISHING
Unit 3, Tristar Centre, Star Road, Partridge Green,
West Sussex RH13 8RA